Published by Ice House Books

Copyright © 2020 Ice House Books
Designed by Smart Design Studio

Ice House Books is an imprint of Half Moon Bay Limited
The Ice House, 124 Walcot Street, Bath, BA1 5BG
www.icehousebooks.co.uk

ISBN 978-1-912867-84-4

Printed in China

LOVE IN
A MUG

FOR THE HANGRY ONE YOU LOVE

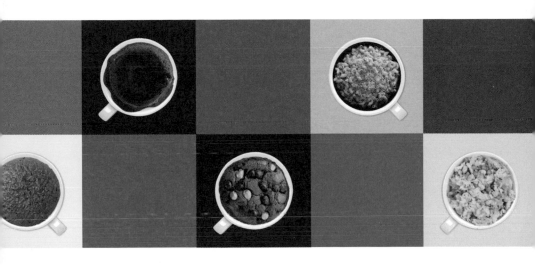

ICE HOUSE BOOKS

Funfetti
Mug Cake

INGREDIENTS

4 tbsp plain flour

¼ tsp baking powder

2 tsp caster sugar

3 tbsp milk

½ tbsp vegetable oil

½ tsp vanilla extract

1½ tsp colourful sprinkles, plus extra to decorate

METHOD

1. Mix the flour, baking powder and sugar in your mug. Add the milk, vegetable oil and vanilla extract and mix until smooth.

2. Stir in the sprinkles so they're distributed throughout the cake batter.

3. Microwave for one minute or until completely cooked. Leave to cool, top with sprinkles, then tuck in!

#1

Chocolate *Peanut Butter* Cake

INGREDIENTS

3 tbsp plain flour
2 tbsp caster sugar
1½ tbsp cocoa powder
¼ tsp baking powder
pinch of salt
3 tbsp milk
1½ tbsp vegetable oil
1 tbsp peanut butter

FOR THOSE **TREAT-YOURSELF** MOMENTS

METHOD

1. Grab your mug and add the flour, sugar, cocoa powder, baking powder and salt. Mix them together.

2. Add the milk, vegetable oil and peanut butter and whisk with a fork until smooth.

3. Cook in the microwave for 1–1½ minutes or until cooked all the way through, and serve!

#2

Pumpkin Pie

WHEN IN OCTOBER, IT WOULD BE RUDE NOT TO

INGREDIENTS

2 tbsp pumpkin purée

1 large free-range egg

2 tbsp brown sugar

1 tsp pumpkin pie spice (or **⅓ tsp** each of cinnamon, ginger, nutmeg)

pinch of salt

1 tbsp milk

½ tsp vanilla extract

2 digestives or ginger biscuits

whipped cream to decorate

METHOD

1. Whisk together the pumpkin purée, egg, sugar, spice, salt, milk and vanilla extract in a small bowl until smooth.

2. Crush the biscuits into the bottom of your mug and pour the pumpkin pie mixture on top.

3. Microwave for 1½–2 minutes or until completely cooked. Allow to cool and top with whipped cream. Mmm!

#3

Red Velvet cake

INGREDIENTS

4 **tbsp** plain flour
2 **tbsp** caster sugar
½ **tbsp** cocoa powder
⅛ **tsp** bicarbonate of soda
3 **tbsp** milk
½ **tbsp** vegetable oil
⅛ **tsp** vinegar
¼ **tsp** red food colouring

FOR THE ICING:

1 **tbsp** cream cheese
1 **tbsp** butter
2½ **tbsp** icing sugar

WHO KNEW A MEAL IN A MUG COULD BE SO LUXURIOUS?

METHOD

1. Mix the dry cake ingredients in your mug. Add the milk, oil, vinegar and food colouring, then mix until smooth.

2. Cook in the microwave for one minute or until completely cooked. Remove and allow the cake to fully cool.

3. In a bowl, mix the cream cheese and butter then sift in the icing sugar. Whip until light and fluffy, decorate the cake and enjoy!

#4

Peach Cobbler

INGREDIENTS

1 peach, peeled and chopped
4 tbsp plain flour
1 tbsp caster sugar
¼ tsp baking powder
pinch of cinnamon
pinch of salt
2 tbsp butter, melted

2 tbsp milk
1 scoop of ice cream for garnish

YOUR GRANNY WOULD BE IMPRESSED!

METHOD

1. Add the peach slices to your mug.

2. In a bowl, combine the flour, sugar, baking powder, cinnamon and salt.

3. Add the melted butter and milk to the flour mixture and mix until smooth. Pour the batter over the peaches.

3. Microwave for 1–1½ minutes at 30 second intervals or until fully cooked. Top with ice cream and serve!

#5

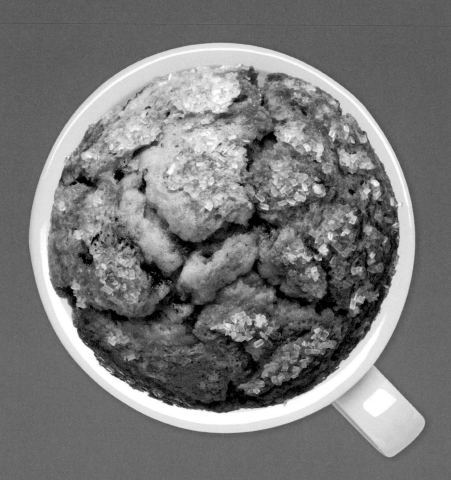

Eggless
Blueberry Cake

INGREDIENTS

6 tbsp plain flour
½ tsp baking powder
2 tbsp butter, melted
2½ tbsp caster sugar
2 tbsp milk
½ tsp vanilla extract
small handful of blueberries

A SATURDAY AFTERNOON TREAT...

METHOD

1. Mix the flour and baking powder together in a bowl. In a separate bowl, whisk together the butter, sugar, milk and vanilla extract. Pour the wet ingredients over the flour mixture and combine until smooth.

2. Stir in the blueberries and add the batter into your mug (only fill halfway, as the cake rises quite a bit).

3. Microwave for one minute or until fully cooked. Delicious!

#6

Oreo® Cake

INGREDIENTS

2 tbsp butter
1 tbsp caster sugar
15 g (½ oz) milk chocolate
1 large free-range egg
2 tbsp single cream
1 tsp vanilla extract
4 tbsp plain flour

YOUR
FAVOURITE
BISCUIT...

TRANSFORMED!

½ tsp baking powder
3 Oreos®, broken (plus 1 extra, broken, for garnish)

METHOD

1. In your mug, melt the butter, sugar and chocolate for 30 seconds. Beat until smooth and allow to cool slightly.

2. One by one, whisk in the egg, cream and vanilla extract. Mix the flour and baking powder in a separate bowl then add them to the mug. Gently stir in the broken Oreos®.

3. Cook in the microwave for 1½ minutes or until cooked all the way through. Allow to cool for one minute, garnish with the extra Oreo® then tuck in!

Carrot Cake

INGREDIENTS

4 tbsp plain flour

2 tbsp brown sugar

¼ tsp baking powder

¼ tsp cinnamon

¼ tsp nutmeg

1 tbsp butter

4 tbsp milk

2 tbsp carrots, grated

FOR THE ICING:

1½ tbsp cream cheese

1½ tbsp butter

3 tbsp icing sugar

YOU'RE GOING TO WANT TO PICK YOUR LARGEST MUG FOR THIS DELIGHT

METHOD

1. Mix the flour, sugar, baking powder, cinnamon and nutmeg in your mug. Add the butter, milk and carrots. Mix well.

2. Microwave for 1–1½ minutes or until fully cooked.

3. In a bowl, mix the cream cheese and butter then sift in the icing sugar. Whip until light and fluffy, decorate the cake and add a carrot decoration if you're feeling fancy!

Sticky Toffee
Pudding

INGREDIENTS

FOR THE CAKE:

3 tbsp plain flour
¼ tsp baking powder
1 tbsp brown sugar
pinch of salt
1 tbsp butter, softened
2 tbsp milk

FOR THE ICING:

3 tbsp maple syrup
1 tbsp water

THE ULTIMATE DESSERT FOR A COSY NIGHT-IN

METHOD

1. In your mug, mix together the flour and baking powder. Add the sugar, salt and butter and mix with a fork, then pour in the milk and stir until smooth.

2. In a small bowl, mix together the maple syrup and water until smooth. Spoon the mixture over the batter.

3. Microwave for one minute or until the cake is fully cooked. Allow to cool and serve!

Chocolate Orange Cake

INGREDIENTS

6 tbsp plain flour
¼ tsp baking powder
3 tbsp ground almonds
3 tbsp caster sugar
2 tbsp butter, melted
¼ tsp salt
1 large free-range egg
1½ tbsp dark chocolate chips

1 tsp orange essence
icing sugar to dust
orange zest for garnish

ORANGE IS FRUIT, SO IT'S HEALTHY RIGHT?

METHOD

1. Grab your mug and combine the flour, baking powder and ground almonds. Add the sugar, butter, salt and egg and mix until smooth. Stir in the chocolate chips and orange essence.

2. Microwave for two minutes until the cake is completely cooked. Allow to cool then garnish with a dusting of icing sugar and orange zest. It's time to indulge!

#10

Apple *Crumble*

HEARTY

GOODNESS

WITHOUT THE

EFFORT.

1 tbsp butter
1 tbsp oats
2 tbsp caster sugar
2 tbsp plain flour
½ apple, diced
1 tbsp water
1 tsp lemon juice

pinch of cinnamon
1 tbsp caster sugar
½ tsp vanilla extract

METHOD

1. Mix together the butter, oats, 2 tablespoons of sugar and flour in a small bowl.

2. In your mug, mix together the apple, water, lemon juice, cinnamon, 1 tablespoon of sugar and vanilla extract. Microwave for three minutes. Spoon the crumble oat mixture on top of the apple mixture.

3. Microwave for an additional 2½ minutes or until completely cooked. Allow to cool and enjoy!

#11

Cinnamon Roll

INGREDIENTS

FOR THE CAKE:

4 tbsp plain flour

1 tbsp caster sugar

¼ tsp baking powder

⅛ tsp cinnamon

½ tbsp vegetable oil

3 tbsp milk

FOR THE CINNAMON SWIRL:

1½ tbsp brown sugar   **⅛ tsp** cinnamon

½ tbsp unsalted butter

FOR THE ICING:

1 tbsp icing sugar   water, as needed

METHOD

1. Add the flour, sugar, baking powder and cinnamon to your mug and mix. Add the oil and milk, mix until smooth then pour half into a separate bowl.

2. In a small microwave-safe bowl, mix together the cinnamon swirl ingredients and microwave for 20–30 seconds until the butter melts. Stir well.

3. Use a spoon to pour a cinnamon swirl onto the cake batter in the mug. Pour the cake batter set aside in the bowl on top, then pour another swirl on top of that.

4. Microwave for one minute or until the cake is fully cooked.

5. Make your icing by adding a little water to the icing sugar and mixing until it's pourable (but not too runny). Drizzle it over the cake and serve!

#12

Lemon and Poppy Seed Cake

FEELING A LITTLE CREATIVE?

6 tbsp plain flour

2½ tbsp caster sugar

¼ tsp baking powder

3 tbsp milk

1 tbsp lemon juice

2 tbsp salted butter, melted

½ tsp vanilla extract

½ tsp poppy seeds

METHOD

1. In a small bowl, whisk together the flour, sugar and baking powder until fully combined.

2. Mix in the milk, lemon juice, butter, vanilla and poppy seeds until smooth.

3. Pour the batter into your mug and microwave for 1½ minutes until the cake is cooked. Allow to cool and tuck in!

Banana Cake

BREAKFAST?

DINNER?

NO ONE'S

JUDGING

3 tbsp self-raising flour

1 tbsp caster sugar

2 tbsp brown sugar

1 tsp vanilla extract

1 large free-range egg

1 tbsp olive oil

1 tbsp milk

1 ripe banana, mashed

METHOD

1. In your mug, mix together the flour, both sugars and the vanilla extract. Add the egg and mix again. Stir in the oil, milk and banana until fully combined.

2 Microwave for 2½ minutes until the cake is fully cooked. Allow to cool and serve!

Victoria Sponge

INGREDIENTS

A CLASSIC, IN MINUTES

2 tbsp butter, melted
1 large free-range egg
2 tbsp milk
1 tsp vanilla extract
4 tbsp caster sugar
6 tbsp self-raising flour
¼ tsp baking powder

pinch of salt
2 tbsp strawberry jam

METHOD

1. In your mug, whisk together the butter and egg.

2. Stir in the milk, vanilla and sugar.

3. In a bowl, mix the flour, baking powder and salt. Add them to the wet ingredients and mix with a fork until smooth.

4. Microwave for 1½ minutes or until the cake is completely cooked. Allow to cool before spreading on the jam. You could also add a scoop of ice cream and fresh strawberries to top it off!

#15

White **Chocolate** and **Raspberry** Cake

NOT YOUR AVERAGE CHOCOLATE CAKE

INGREDIENTS

50 g (2 oz) white chocolate, chopped

1 tbsp butter

1 tbsp milk

1 tbsp sugar

⅛ tsp vanilla extract

3 tbsp plain flour

⅛ tsp baking powder

pinch of salt

50 g (2 oz) raspberries

white chocolate for garnish, grated

METHOD

1. Mix the white chocolate and butter together in your mug. Microwave for 30 seconds, until both the chocolate and butter are fully melted. Stir to combine.

2. Mix in the milk, sugar and vanilla. Mix the flour, baking powder and salt in a separate bowl then combine with the wet mixture until smooth. Stir in the raspberries (leave a few spare to garnish).

3. Microwave for 1½ minutes or until the cake is fully cooked. Allow to cool, garnish with the spare raspberries and grated white chocolate, then serve!

#16

French Toast

INGREDIENTS

1 tsp butter, melted
3 tbsp milk
1 tsp maple syrup
¼ tsp cinnamon
¼ tsp vanilla extract
pinch of nutmeg
1 large free-range egg
handful of bread pieces
handful of fresh berries for garnish

ONE FOR THOSE SUNDAY HANGOVERS

METHOD

1. In your mug, add the butter, milk, maple syrup, cinnamon, vanilla, nutmeg and egg, then whisk until fully combined.

2. Add the bread pieces and gently stir until they have absorbed the liquid.

3. Microwave for 1–1½ minutes until fully cooked and the mixture is set. Garnish with fresh berries!

#17

Vegan *Brownie*

INGREDIENTS

2 tbsp water

2 tbsp coconut or vegetable oil

½ tsp vanilla extract

4 tbsp sugar

2 tbsp cocoa powder

4 tbsp plain flour

¼ tsp salt

METHOD

1. Combine the water, oil and vanilla extract in your mug. Mix in the sugar and cocoa powder, then add the flour and salt, mixing again.

Salted Caramel Cake

INGREDIENTS

3 tbsp butter, melted

1 large free-range egg, beaten

3 tbsp milk

4 tbsp plain flour

3 tbsp brown sugar

½ tsp baking powder

½ tsp salt

2 tbsp salted caramel

nuts for garnish

YOUR MOUTH IS WATERING...

METHOD

1. In your mug, mix the butter, egg and milk with a fork until combined. Combine the flour, sugar, baking powder and salt in a separate bowl, then add to the wet ingredients and mix until smooth.

2. Add one tablespoon of salted caramel on top of the mixture and microwave for one minute or until fully cooked.

3. Garnish with chopped nuts and drizzle over the remaining tablespoon of salted caramel, then serve!

Triple
Chocolate Cake

INGREDIENTS

4 tbsp plain flour

½ tsp bicarbonate of soda

3 tbsp sugar

1 tbsp cocoa powder

1 tbsp coconut or vegetable oil

3 tbsp milk

½ tsp vanilla extract

pinch of salt

2 tbsp mix of dark, milk and white chocolate chips, plus extra for garnish

METHOD

1. Grab your mug, add the flour and bicarbonate of soda, and mix well. Add the rest of the ingredients (except the chocolate chips) and mix until smooth. Stir in the chocolate chips.

2. Microwave for 1½ minutes or until fully cooked. Garnish with the extra chocolate chips and microwave for a further 10 seconds. Allow to cool and enjoy!

#20

Macaroni Cheese

INGREDIENTS

30 g (1 oz) macaroni pasta
100 ml (3½ fl oz) milk
½ tbsp butter
4 tbsp cheddar cheese, grated
salt and pepper
toasted breadcrumbs for garnish

METHOD

1. Add the pasta and milk to your mug.

2. Microwave for 2–3 minutes, until the pasta is fully cooked.

3. Stir in the butter and add the cheese. Season to taste then microwave for 30 seconds.

4. Stir well and serve with toasted breadcrumbs on top for an added crunch!

Egg Fried Rice

INGREDIENTS

200 g (7 oz) cooked rice

2 tbsp frozen peas

2 tbsp spring onions, chopped

1 large free-range egg

1 tbsp soy sauce

½ tsp sesame oil

½ tsp onion powder

METHOD

1. Pop the rice in your mug, then add the peas and spring onions on top.

2. Cover the mug with cling film and puncture one or two holes using a knife. Microwave for 1¼ minutes.

3. In a small bowl, beat the egg, then add the soy sauce, sesame oil and onion powder. Pour the egg mix into the mug and stir all the ingredients together.

4. Re-cover the mug with the cling film and microwave for 1½ minutes or until completely cooked. Stir and leave to stand, then serve!

Omelette

1 tsp olive oil

2 large free-range eggs

1 tbsp milk

1 tbsp cheddar cheese, grated

1 tbsp bell pepper, chopped

1 tsp chives, chopped

salt and pepper

PERFECT FOR A QUICK LUNCH

METHOD

1. Grease your mug with the oil.

2. Crack the eggs into the mug with the milk and beat with a fork.

3. Add the grated cheese, bell pepper, and chives. Season with salt and pepper and stir well until mixed.

4. Microwave for 30 second intervals, stirring in between until the omelette is cooked and fully set. Tuck in!

#23

Quiche

INGREDIENTS

1 large free-range egg

1½ tbsp milk

1 tsp butter, melted

salt and pepper

4 small tomatoes, halved

1 slice of bread, torn into small pieces

1 tbsp cheddar cheese, grated

1 tsp chives, chopped

METHOD

1. In your mug, mix together the egg, milk and butter, and season with salt and pepper.

2. Add the tomatoes, bread, cheese and chives to the mixture until fully incorporated.

3. Cook in the microwave for one minute until the egg is fully cooked, and serve!

#24

Pizza

INGREDIENTS

4 tbsp plain flour
⅛ tsp baking powder
¹⁄₁₆ tsp bicarbonate of soda
pinch of salt
½ tsp Italian seasoning
3 tbsp milk
1 tbsp vegetable oil
1 tbsp mozzarella cheese
¼ tomato, sliced

pepperoni slices
salt and pepper

METHOD

1. Mix the flour, baking powder, bicarbonate of soda, salt, seasoning, milk and oil in your mug, until smooth.

2. Add the mozzarella, tomato slices and pepperoni on top of the batter.

3. Cook in the microwave for 1–1½ minutes or until fully cooked. Garnish with a basil leaf if you wish, season with salt and pepper, and serve!

#25

Burrito

INGREDIENTS

1 large tortilla
2 large free-range eggs
2 tbsp black beans
2 tbsp cheddar cheese, grated
2 tbsp spring onions, chopped
salt and pepper

2 tbsp avocado, chopped
2 tbsp peppers, chopped
2 tbsp sweetcorn

METHOD

1. Press the fresh tortilla into your mug so it lines the mug.

2. Crack the eggs into the mug and whisk with a fork, being careful not to tear the tortilla.

3. Add the beans, cheese and spring onions. Season with salt and pepper, then mix everything together.

4. Microwave for 1½ minutes until the eggs are cooked. Allow to sit for a few minutes then top with the avocado, peppers and sweetcorn. It's even better with sour cream and salsa on top!

Cheese and Bacon Muffin

INGREDIENTS

4 tbsp plain flour

½ tsp baking powder

½ tsp onion powder (optional)

pinch of salt

½ tbsp butter

3½ tbsp milk

1 tbsp cooked bacon, chopped

1 tbsp cheddar cheese, grated

AN ON-THE-GO LUNCH FOR YOUR TRUE LOVE

METHOD

1. In your mug, mix together the flour, baking powder, onion powder (if using) and salt until fully combined. Rub in the butter until it forms a breadcrumb texture.

2. Stir in the milk, bacon and cheese until a batter is formed, then microwave for 45 seconds or until completely cooked. Tuck in!

#27

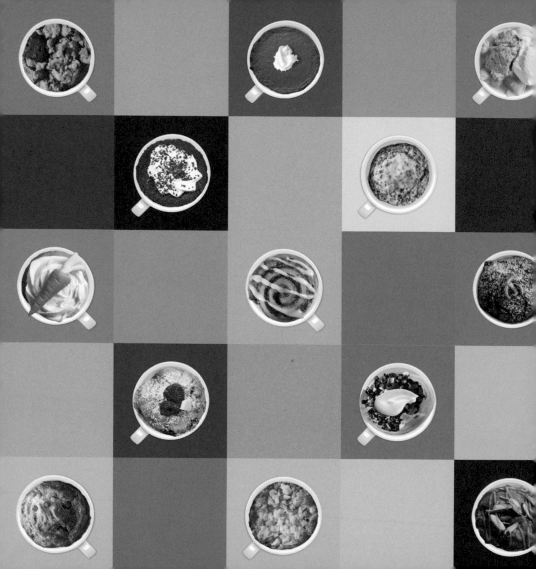